WHAT DO YOU WANT TO DO BEFORE YOU DIE?

MOVING, UNEXPECTED, AND INSPIRING ANSWERS TO LIFE'S MOST IMPORTANT QUESTION

THE BURIED LIFE

Ben Nemtin, Dave Lingwood, Duncan Penn, and Jonnie Penn

ARTISAN | NEW YORK

BLAH
BLAH
BLAH!

Library of Congress Cataloging-in-Publication
data is on file.

ISBN 978-1-57965-878-6

Art direction/design: Kevin Brainard
Design assistant: Joanne O'Neill

Cover and interior illustrations by
Christopher Brand, Matthew Dorfman,
Matthew Hollister, Oliver Munday, Joanne
O'Neill, and Jeffrey Scher

Photos courtesy of Shila Farahani (page 4)
and Johnny Miller (pages 68, 133, 137, 147, 169).
Used by permission.

Artisan books are available at special discounts
when purchased in bulk for premiums and sales
promotions as well as for fund-raising
or educational use. Special editions or book
excerpts also can be created to specification.
For details, contact the Special Sales Director
at the address below, or send an e-mail to
specialmarkets@workman.com.

For speaking engagements, contact
speakersbureau@workman.com.

Published by Artisan
A division of Workman Publishing Co., Inc.
225 Varick Street
New York, NY 10014-4381
artisanbooks.com

Artisan is a registered trademark of
Workman Publishing Co., Inc.

Originally published in slightly different form
by Artisan in 2012.

Published simultaneously in Canada by
Thomas Allen & Son, Limited

Printed in China

10 9 8 7 6 5 4 3 2 1

THIS BOOK IS DEDICATED TO THE MEMORY
OF MIKEY KALAMAR, WHO TOOK HIS OWN LIFE
AT THE AGE OF SEVENTEEN. WE URGE YOU TO
REMEMBER THAT PAIN IS NOT ALWAYS VISIBLE
AND THAT YOU ARE ALWAYS LOVED.

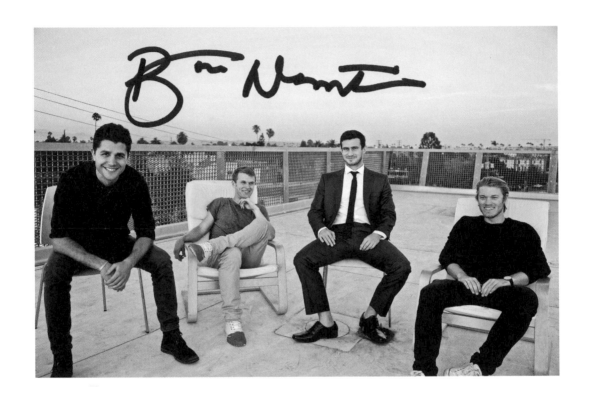

BEN NEMTIN, JONNIE PENN, DAVE LINGWOOD, AND
DUNCAN PENN STARTED THE BURIED LIFE IN
A GARAGE IN 2006. THEIR GOAL IS TO
COMPLETE A LIST OF 100 THINGS TO DO BEFORE THEY
DIE AND TO HELP AND ENCOURAGE OTHERS
TO DO THE SAME.

100 THINGS TO DO BEFORE I DIE

1. ~~Open the six o'clock news~~
2. ~~Lead a parade~~
3. ~~Get a tattoo~~
4. ~~Start a dance in a public place~~
5. ~~Go down a mountain on a longboard~~
6. ~~Attend a party at the Playboy Mansion~~
7. ~~Plant a tree~~
8. ~~Ride a bull~~
9. ~~Destroy a computer~~
10. ~~Learn to fly~~
11. ~~Get a college degree~~
12. ~~Kick a field goal~~
13. ~~Help someone build a house~~
14. ~~Grow a mustache~~
15. Get on the cover of *Rolling Stone*
16. ~~Drive across North America~~
17. ~~Start a huge wave~~
18. ~~Tell a joke on late-night television~~
19. ~~Write a bestselling book~~
20. ~~Get a song we've written on the radio~~
21. ~~Become a licensed minister~~
22. ~~Approach the most beautiful girl you've ever seen and kiss her~~
23. ~~Learn how to play an instrument~~
24. ~~Go to a rock concert dressed all in leather~~
25. ~~Solve a crime or capture a fugitive~~
26. Tell a judge: "You want the truth? You can't handle the truth!"
27. ~~Give a stranger a $100 bill~~
28. ~~Send a message in a bottle~~
29. ~~Scream at the top of your lungs~~
30. ~~Make a big donation to charity~~
31. ~~Cut a ribbon at a major opening~~
32. ~~Get something named after you~~
33. ~~Compete in a Krump competition~~
34. ~~Pay for someone's groceries~~
35. ~~Sing the national anthem to a packed stadium~~
36. ~~Throw the first pitch at a major-league baseball game~~
37. ~~Win and yell "Bingo!" at a bingo hall~~
38. ~~Kiss the Stanley Cup~~
39. ~~Stand under a plane while it lands~~
40. ~~Make the front page of the newspaper~~
41. ~~Make a toast at a stranger's wedding~~
42. ~~Spend a night in jail~~
43. ~~Become a knight for a day~~
44. ~~Catch something and eat it~~
45. ~~Sleep in a haunted house~~
46. ~~Do a sketch with Will Ferrell~~
47. ~~Get in *The Guinness Book of World Records*~~
48. ~~Accept a dare~~
49. ~~Take a stranger out for dinner~~
50. ~~Streak a stadium~~ and get away with it
51. ~~Climb a large mountain~~
52. ~~Go on a blind date~~
53. ~~Make a TV show~~
54. ~~Donate blood~~
55. Kiss Rachel McAdams
56. ~~Write an article for a major publication~~
57. ~~Spend a week in silence~~
58. ~~See a dead body~~
59. ~~Ask out the girl of your dreams~~
60. ~~Go paragliding~~
61. ~~Paint a mural~~
62. ~~Protest something~~
63. ~~Run a successful business~~
64. ~~Visit Folsom Prison~~
65. ~~Learn how to sail~~
66. ~~Walk the red carpet~~
67. ~~Make an important speech~~
68. ~~Swim with sharks~~
69. ~~Smash a guitar onstage~~
70. ~~Compete in a soapbox derby~~
71. ~~Take kids on a shopping spree~~
72. ~~Throw a surprise party~~
73. ~~Make a music video~~
74. ~~Help deliver a baby~~
75. ~~Make a million bucks~~
76. ~~Go dogsledding~~
77. ~~Go to Burning Man~~
78. ~~Fall in love~~
79. ~~Dance with Ellen DeGeneres~~
80. ~~Meet the Lonely Island dudes~~
81. ~~Tour with a major band~~
82. ~~Win an award~~
83. ~~Street perform and make $100~~
84. ~~Run a marathon~~
85. ~~Throw the most badass party ever~~
86. ~~Teach an elementary school class~~
87. Pay off our parents' mortgages
88. ~~Survive on a deserted island~~
89. Experience zero gravity
90. ~~Ride a roller coaster~~
91. Get married ~~(in Vegas)~~
92. ~~Learn how to surf~~
93. ~~Ride through the desert in a dune buggy~~
94. ~~Party with a rock star~~
95. ~~Play ball with the president~~
96. ~~Run a lemonade stand~~
97. ~~Get in a fight~~
98. ~~Race horses~~
99. Host *Saturday Night Live*
100. Go to space

"WHAT DO YOU WANT TO DO BEFORE YOU DIE?"

OUR STORY

What began as a two-week road trip with four friends became a movement. By following our dreams, the four of us—Jonnie, Ben, Dave, and Duncan—inadvertently challenged the world to grab hold of life. We stumbled upon the simple idea that by doing what you love, you inspire others to do the same.

We were desperate for meaning. Ben had been hit by a crippling depression that forced him to drop out of college. Duncan was devastated by the death of his friend who had drowned, and his brother, Jonnie, was struggling to come to terms with their parents' sudden divorce. Dave had gained forty-five pounds in his first semester of college and was stuck in a downward spiral. We were all lost, detached from the promise of growing up; ill prepared for adulthood, without even the vocabulary to express it. In an attempt to feel alive, we came up with a plan to hit the open road and attempt to live out one hundred of our wildest dreams. For each item we accomplished, we agreed to help a total stranger do something they had always dreamed about doing.

In the summer of 2006, the four of us borrowed a 1977 RV, bought a secondhand camera so we could film the journey, and hit the road for two weeks to tackle our list. It was a harebrained scheme, hatched from a potent mix of ambition and disillusionment. What happened next was an unexpected mixture of luck and magic. People began to hear about our project and wanted to help. Some of them stepped up to help us complete our bucket list; others reached out asking for help accomplishing their own biggest dreams. We decided to call our mission The Buried Life, after a 150-year-old poem by Matthew Arnold that precisely articulated our feelings—that we were buried.

BUT OFTEN, IN THE WORLD'S MOST
CROWDED STREETS,
BUT OFTEN, IN THE DIN OF STRIFE,
THERE RISES AN UNSPEAKABLE DESIRE
AFTER THE KNOWLEDGE OF OUR
BURIED LIFE...

The two-week road trip never truly ended. Adventures and life lessons continued to unfold, year after year, and we uncovered a growing sense of purpose. We found that helping others had a lasting impact, sometimes greater than that of accomplishing our own goals, and—most important—that everything seems impossible until it's done.

The Buried Life continues to ask the question "What do you want to do before you die?" and to tackle that list to prove that anyone can do anything.

WHY WE WROTE THIS BOOK

The way we live today, it's easy to get buried by the everyday grind; to put your dreams on the back burner until next year. The greatest way to unbury your dreams is to write them down. Make them tangible; make them real. Breathe into your deepest hopes and slowly stitch together exactly what you desire, then watch the world around you change. When you take an idea hibernating in your mind and scrawl it on paper, you're actually making the first move toward completion. Next, talk about your list—give people a chance to help you make your dreams a reality. The sense of accountability created by sharing your dreams will help propel you forward. Push through the fear of what other people might think, because if you don't, no one can help you. Support will appear from the most unexpected places if you share your goals with passion and authenticity.

When you create your list, be brave and ambitious. Audacious goals will fuel you like a self-fulfilling prophecy. Tim Ferriss says it well: "Ninety-nine percent of the people in the world are convinced they are incapable of achieving great things, so they aim for the mediocre. The level of competition is thus fiercest for 'realistic' goals." You don't need to know how to accomplish your most audacious goal; you just need to have the bravery to take the first step. You can figure out your second step once you're there.

Just like we were triggered in our moments of darkness, we hope that the dreams and words filling these pages will ignite part of you, and halt you long enough to sincerely think about what is important to you. It's easy to think about what's important to others, but rarely do we truly listen to our gut and our heart, and that is where a bucket list should grow. If nothing in the world were impossible, what would you do? Even if it *is* impossible, what do you want to do before you die? Our dream is that you'll write your list with honesty and ambition and begin living out your own dreams, because just by doing so you will inspire others to follow.

—Ben, Dave, Duncan, and Jonnie

THE FOLLOWING LIST ITEMS WERE CHOSEN FROM TENS OF THOUSANDS OF ANSWERS TO THE QUESTION "WHAT DO YOU WANT TO DO BEFORE YOU DIE?" THE ITEMS WERE THEN GIVEN TO OUR FAVORITE ARTISTS TO INTERPRET AND BRING TO LIFE.

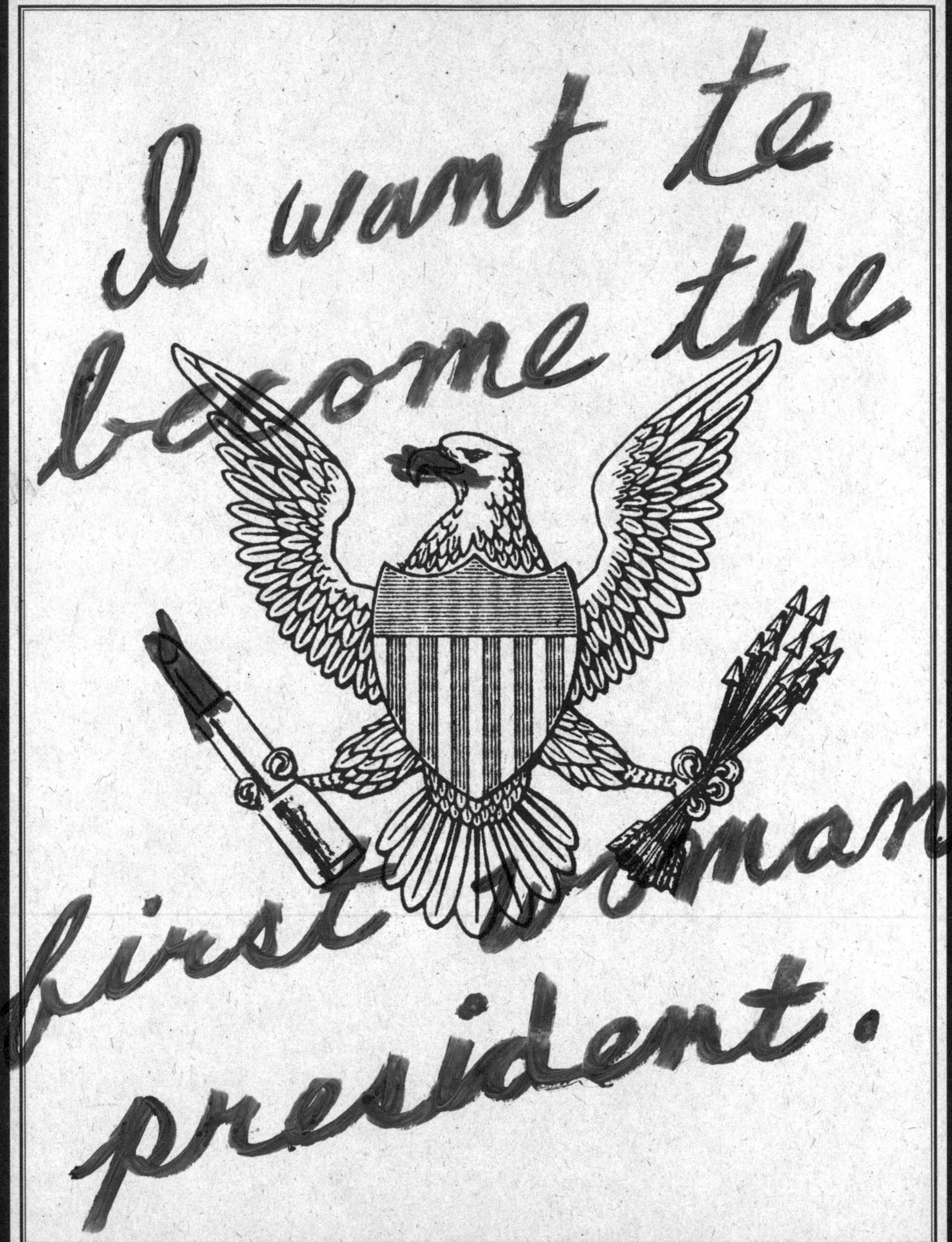
I want to become the first woman president.

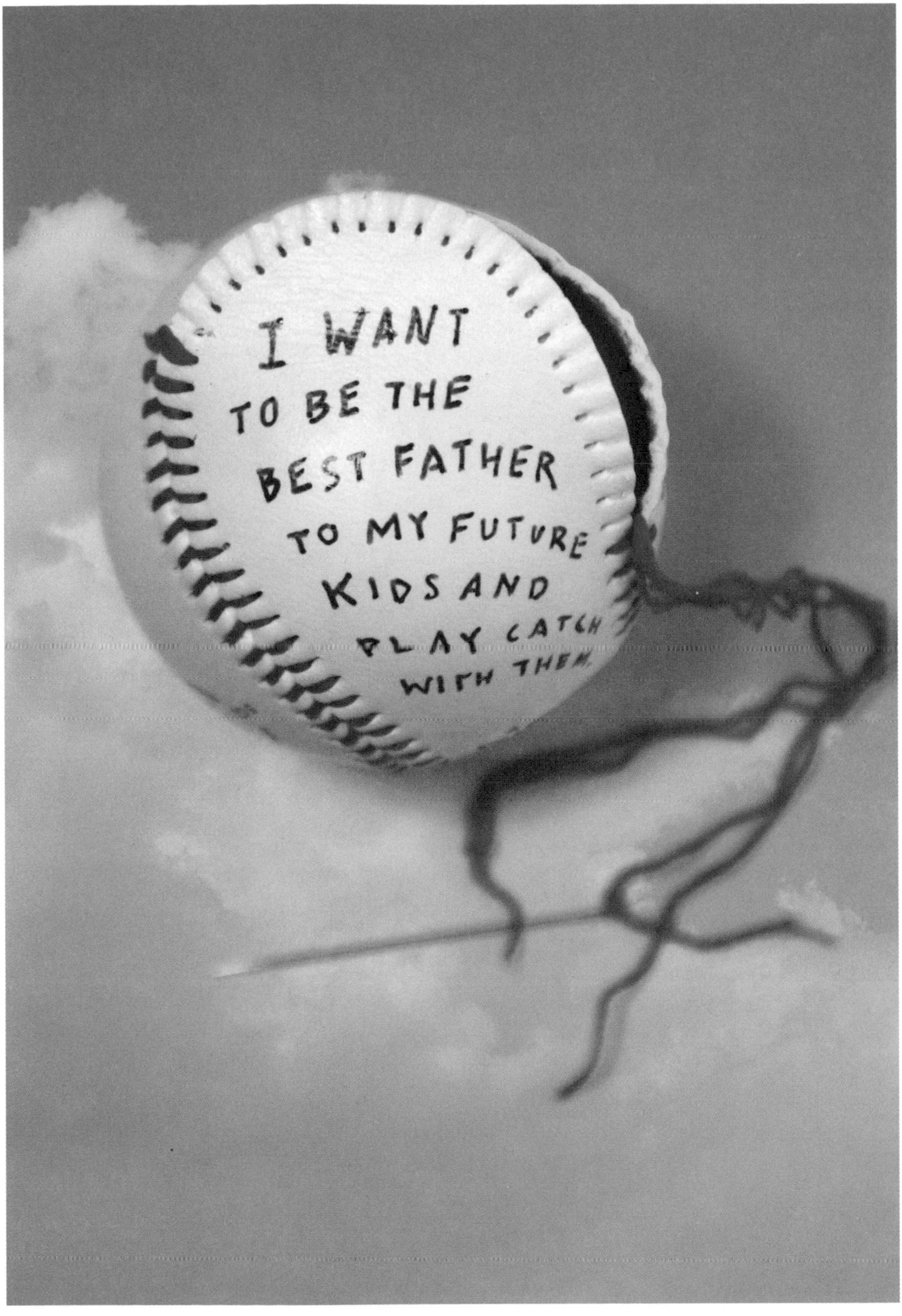
I WANT
TO BE THE
BEST FATHER
TO MY FUTURE
KIDS AND
PLAY CATCH
WITH THEM.

Two years ago, my son was diagnosed with severe autism. I want nothing more than to have my son be treated as an equal.

Before I die I want to hear him say,

"I love you, Mom."

I WANT TO FLY WITH A JETPACK.

-X Axis

X-Axis Zero Sta

15"

Thrust
Unit

139.64"

53.66"

42.16"

18.8'

37.50'

BALLAST

DECODERS
AUTOPILOT
TRANSMITTER

ENVIRONMENT
EQUIP.
RECEIVERS

ALCOHOL

Power
Unit

59.00'

16.83'

LOX

Tail Unit
9.27'

I WANT TO GO AROUND THE WORLD AND FIND **MY OWN** PERSONAL SEVEN WONDERS.

BOTH MY TWIN SISTER AND MY YOUNGER SISTER ARE SUFFERING FROM IT.

I WANT TO START AN ORGANIZATION THAT HELPS TEENS BATTLE DEPRESSION.

I want to forgive my father for all the pain he has caused my family.

"ALL MEN DREAM: BUT NOT EQUALLY. THOSE WHO DREAM BY NIGHT IN THE DUSTY RECESSES OF THEIR MINDS WAKE IN THE DAY TO FIND THAT IT WAS VANITY: BUT THE DREAMERS OF THE DAY ARE DANGEROUS MEN, FOR THEY MAY ACT THEIR DREAM WITH OPEN EYES, TO MAKE IT POSSIBLE."

—T. E. LAWRENCE

Before I die

I want
to learn
how to say
"I love you"
in all
languages

I WANT TO INTERVIEW A KILLER.

Before I die I want to let my English teacher know that she saved my life.

I want to ~~good thos~~
write ~~all kinds of~~
~~big words in a row,~~
~~fill pages with em,~~
~~just keep writing just~~
~~rolling along fast as if~~
~~you can go and~~
~~than when they are~~
~~all put together you~~
~~get~~ a Novel.

I WANT TO BE ABLE TO PAY FOR MY GIRLFRIEND'S COLLEGE SO HER PARENTS CAN'T MAKE HER CHOOSE

BETWEEN COLLEGE AND ME.

Before I
die I want
to understand
why my mom
chooses drugs
over me and
my brother.

I WANT everyone IN parking

TO MOON THE school lot.

I WANT TO SWING FROM A CHANDELIER.

I want to do a
Handstand at
the South Pole
So I can say
I held up the
world.

Before I die I want to smoke a joint on the roof of the White House.

BEFORE I DIE I WANT TO BE A VOICE IN A DISNEY MOVIE.

"I'D RATHER BE HATED FOR WHO I AM
THAN LOVED FOR WHO I'M NOT."

—KURT COBAIN

I WANT TO
HAVE A PARTY WITH
FAKE ALCOHOL...

AND SEE HOW MANY
PEOPLE ACT LIKE
THEY'RE WASTED!

I want to see my mom become sober.

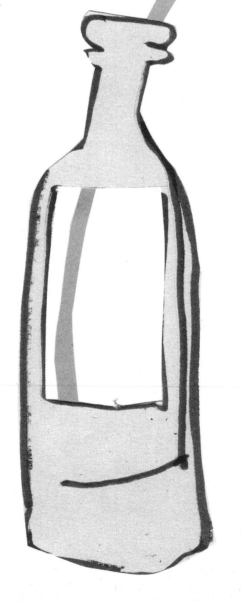

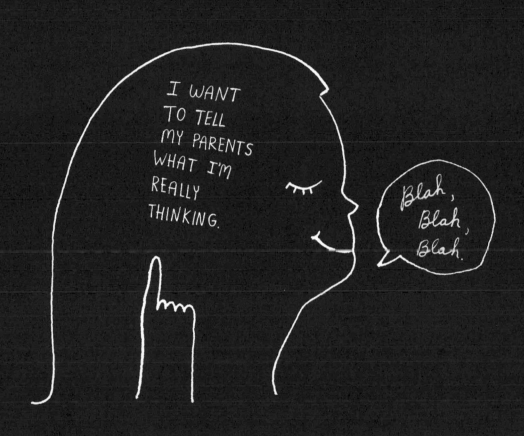

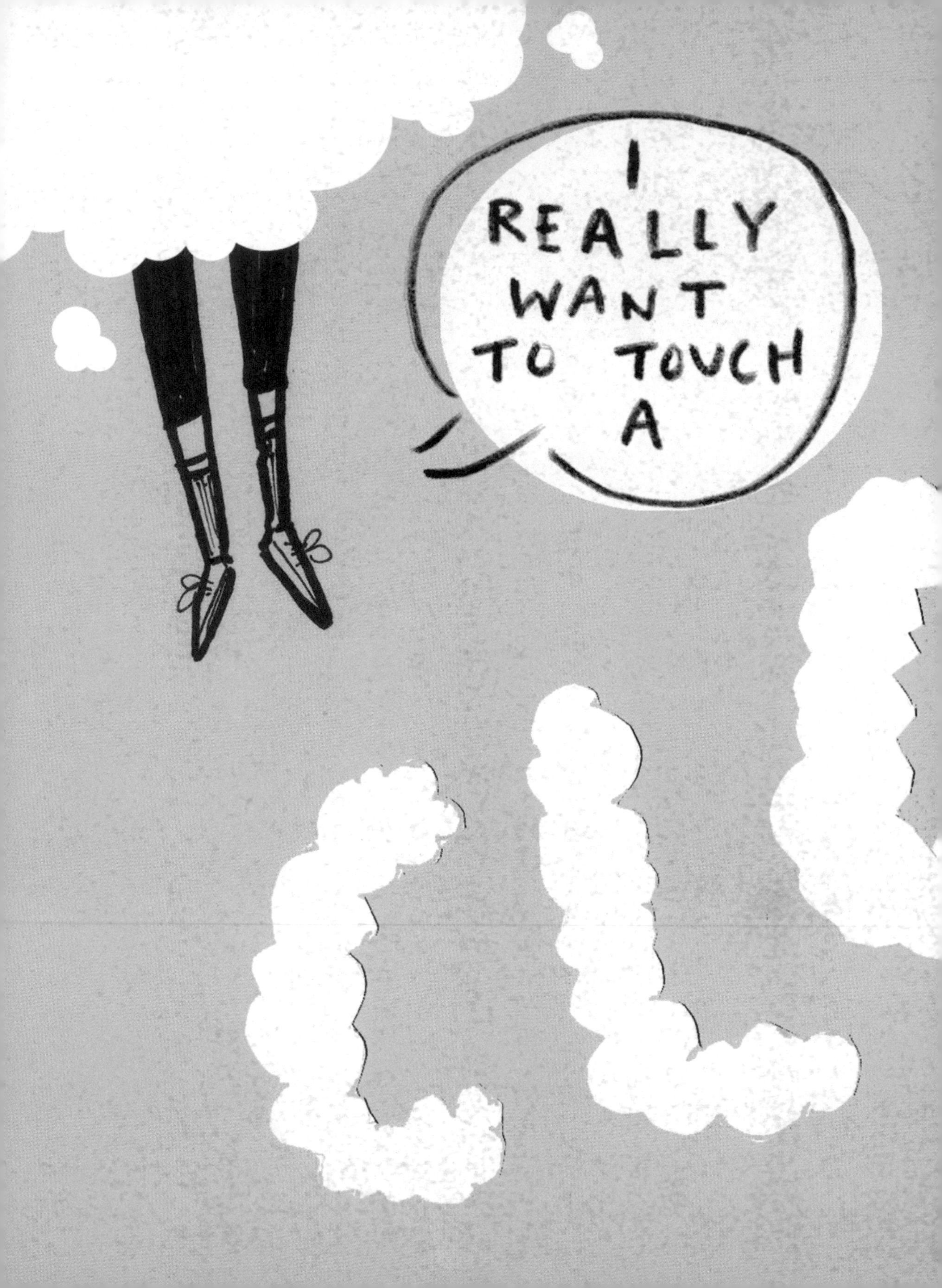
I REALLY WANT TO TOUCH A

I
would
like
to
knock
down

but
with
a
big
crane.

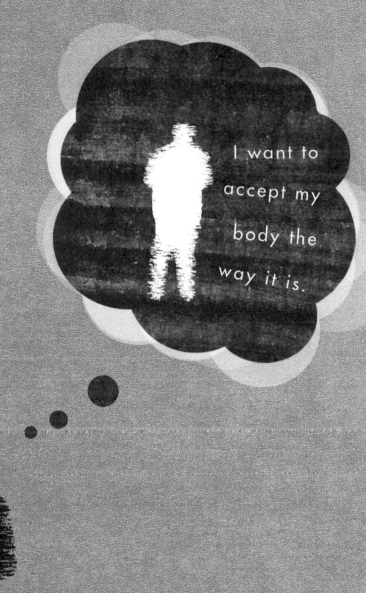

BEN NEMTIN

After high school, my whole world was turned upside down when I was blindsided by a debilitating depression. During my first year at college, I dropped out, I stopped hanging out with my friends, and I stopped playing sports. I had made the U-19 national rugby team and was invited to the World Cup in France, but I said I couldn't play because of an injury. That was a lie. The truth was, I couldn't sleep at night. My anxiety had gotten so bad that I couldn't leave the house. I would pace around the front hall, but I couldn't muster the courage to go out the front door. I remember getting so frightened at night that I couldn't believe the feeling was real.

A group of friends pulled me out of my house and told me I was joining them to live and work in another town for the summer. They didn't give me a choice. Once I was in a new environment, I was forced to start doing things for myself again. I had to get a job, I had to meet new people—I had to leave the cocoon I had spun for myself. Little by little, I slowly started coming out of my fog.

That summer, I learned how to get back up after you hit rock bottom. I learned that if I talked about my struggles, they held less power over me. I realized that I had control over the choices I made and the people I hung out with. From then on, I made a vow to surround myself with people who inspired me. It was a seemingly small shift that had a colossal impact.

I called Jonnie because he was the most inspiring kid I knew. He made movies, so I asked him if he wanted to make one together. Once Jonnie agreed, Dave and Duncan joined shortly after.

We didn't tell anyone what we were up to because we didn't know how to explain it—what we shared was just a feeling. We moved forward without a plan. All we had was a list of one hundred things we wanted to do before we died, the idea to film ourselves tackling the goals on that list during a two-week road trip, an unreliable borrowed RV, and a production company we fabricated to raise money for our camera. I made up a wedding to get time off from work, and we were ready for our journey. The night before we left, we sat on the curb beside the RV arguing about whether we should cancel the trip because if the RV broke down, we didn't have the money to tow it home. We almost didn't leave.

In the beginning, we put items on the list just for a laugh. We pretended we were unstoppable and wrote down whatever popped into our heads. Jonnie called me one day to say we should add "Play Ball with

President Obama" to the list. I laughed because it was the most impossible list item I could think of. Yet somehow, a few years later we found ourselves in the backyard of the White House shooting hoops with the then president. And somehow, "#53: Make a TV Show" and "#19: Write a #1 *New York Times* Bestselling Book" also happened. As Nelson Mandela said, "It always seems impossible until it's done."

We stumbled upon the idea of creating a bucket list at a young age, and it has slowly evolved into a lifestyle of intention. In its simplest form, a bucket list is a record of the most important goals in your life—the things that you are certain will bring you the most joy and fulfillment. Sometimes these goals change over time, but the list itself is simply a device to remind you that your dreams exist. Without a physical reminder, dreams are left unattended and they tend to get buried.

Ben Nemtin is a cofounder of The Buried Life, producer, mental health advocate, and speaker.

I want to know I was a good role model for my little bro.

I WANT TO KAYAK IN A BAY OF BIOLUMINESCENT PLANKTON.

I WANT TO REPAY ALL THE KINDNESS MY FRIENDS HAVE SHOWN ME ALL THEIR LIVES.

I Want To Be a Gypsy

**Before I die
I want to crack
a smile on
one of those
British guards.**

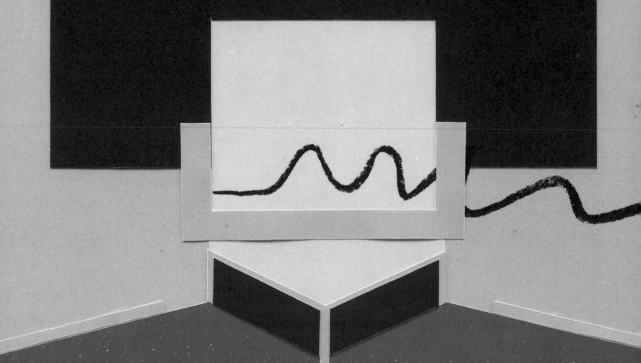

i want to earn the MEDAL of HONOR

during deployment.

Before I die
I want to spread
my father's ashes
in the lake
where he
drowned.

MY father had written short stories his
whole life, but I guess he never thought
they were good enough to submit. Before I die
I want to see at least one of my father's
stories in print.

Short Stories by Dad
Vol. I

I want my mother to go
one day without being in pain.

THANK YOU
THANK YOU
THANK YOU
THANK YOU

I WANT TO TRAVEL THE WORLD,
BAGGING PEOPLE'S GROCERIES.

BEFORE I DIE I WANT

TO WALK A DAY

IN THE SHOES

OF SOMEONE I DON'T

UNDERSTAND.

**"INVEST YOUR MONEY
IN BEAUTIFUL MEMORIES."**

—DUNCAN PENN

I WANT TO TAG
BANKSY WHILE
HE'S SLEEPING.

Before I die

I want to be that

"link" THat introduces

a future

husband and wife.

I want to take my 96-year-old Grandpa, who has been playing piano for 86 years, to see a symphony orchestra.

Before I die I want to meet my long-lost brother. My dad passed away when I was six and my brother was adopted and his name was changed. None of us have seen him since he was eight months old.

I WANT TO PROVE
TO MY DAD
THAT I'M NOT
JUST ANOTHER
LETDOWN AND
DO SOMETHING
WITH MY LIFE.

"OUR DOUBTS ARE TRAITORS, AND MAKE US LOSE THE GOOD WE OFT MIGHT WIN, BY FEARING TO ATTEMPT."

—WILLIAM SHAKESPEARE

I WANT TO BE THE

FIRST GIRL

BASEBALL PLAYER TO

PLAY FOR THE

SAN FRANCISCO

GIANTS.

I WANT
TO SAY
" MEOW "
DURING A
SPEECH.

Before I die I would like To help Find a missing person.

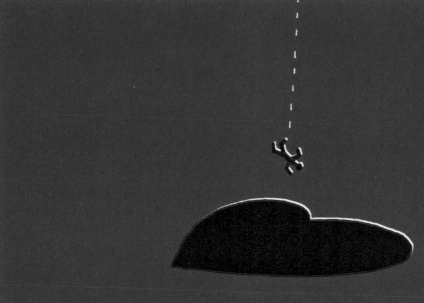

I want to fall in love.

I want to help
the homeless
man who plays
the flute on the
bench outside
our local Safeway.

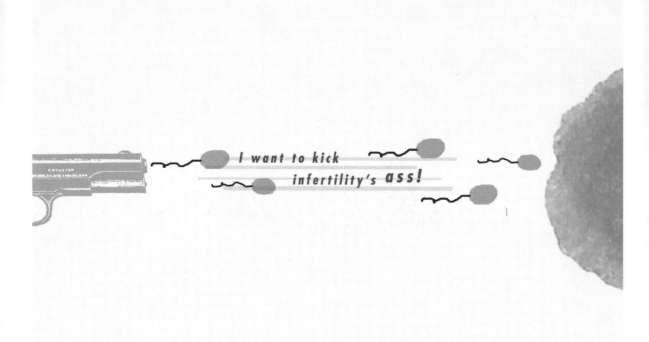

I want to kick infertility's ass!

Before I die
I want Robert De Niro to turn to me
and say,

"YOU TALKIN' TO ME?"

"TODAY IS THE YOUNGEST YOU'LL EVER BE."

—ANONYMOUS

WHITE WOLF SALOON BEER LIST
DRINK YOUR WAY 'ROUND
THE WORLD

Name _____

____ 1. Alaskan Amber- Juneau, Alaska

____ 2. Amstel Light- Amsterdam, Holland

____ 3. Anchor Steam- San Francisco, Ca

____ 4. Moose Drool   Big Sky
____ 5. Summer Honey   Missoula, Montana
____ 6. I.P.A.
____ 7. Troutslayer

____ 8. Bitch Creek- Victor, Idaho

____ 9. Bass Ale- Luton, England

____ 10. Blue Moon   Golden, Co
____ 11. Rising Moon
____ 12. Full Moon/ Honeymoon

____ 13. Dos Equis- Monterey, Mexico

____ 14. Deadguy- New Portland

____ 15. Fat Tire/ Skinny Dip Ft. Collins,Co

____ 16. Fosters- Melbourne, Australia

____ 17. Grolsch- Enschede, Holland

____ 18. Guinness- Dublin,Ireland

____ 19. Harp- New Brunswick, Canada

____ 20. Hamms- Milwaukee, Wisconsin

____ 21. Heineken- Holland

____ 22. Icehouse- Milwaukee

____ 23. Killians Red- Enniscorthy, Ireland

____ 24. Landshark- Jacksonville, Fl

____ 25. Miller- Ft. Worth, Tx

____ 26. Lowenbrau- Munich, Germany

____ 27. Kokannee- Creston, B.C.

____ 28. Keystone- Golden, Co.

____ 29. Leinenkugels Honey
                        Berry
____ 31.   "   Classic Amber
____ 32.   "   Sunset Wh
____ 33.   Summer Shandy
                Chippewa Falls, Wisc.
____ 34. Pabst- Milwaukee

____ 35. Pyramid – Portland, Or

____ 36. Michelob- St. Louis

____ 37. Molson- Toronto

____ 38. Moosehead- New Brunswick

____ 39. Newcastle- Dunston, Eng

____ 40. Old Milwaukee- Milwaukee

____ 41. Pacifico-Mazatlan, Mex

____ 42. Rainer- Irwindale, Ca

____ 43. Red Stripe- Kingston, Jam

____ 44. Rolling Rock- St. Louis

____ 45. 90 Schillings, Ft. Collins

I WANT TO DRINK MY WAY AROUND THE WORLD.

I want to
air-drop
thousands of
flowers over
Times
Square.

I want to be able to help my overweight dad to be healthy again so that he'll live to be my first dance at my WEDDING.

"LIFE HAS BECOME IMMEASURABLY BETTER SINCE I HAVE BEEN FORCED TO STOP TAKING IT SO SERIOUSLY."

—HUNTER S. THOMPSON

Before I die I want to crash a *Wedding* dressed in a dragon costume.

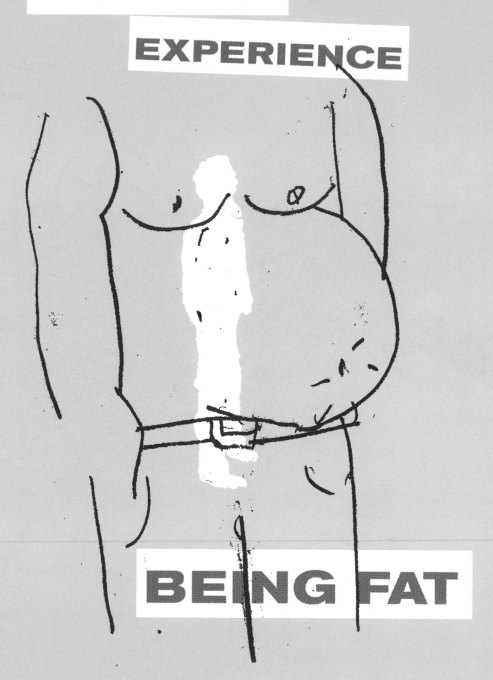

I WANT TO EXPERIENCE BEING FAT FOR A DAY.

I WANT TO MARRY THE LOVE OF MY LIFE.

I WANT TO FREE AN *innocent* MAN FROM JAIL.

I want to longboard down an active volcano.

i want

to be
SOMEBODY

"IF YOU THINK YOU ARE TOO SMALL TO MAKE A DIFFERENCE, TRY SLEEPING WITH A MOSQUITO."

—THE DALAI LAMA

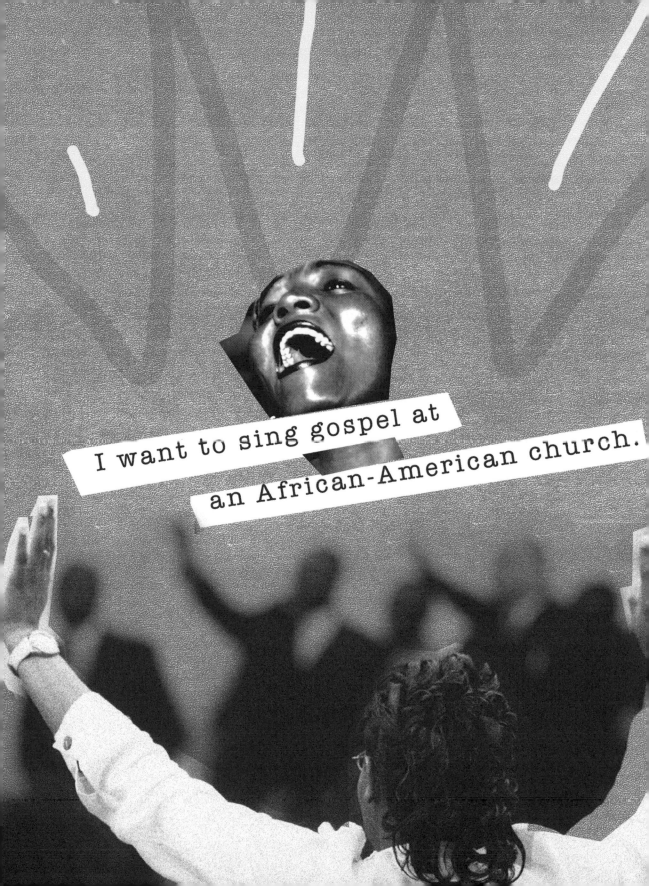

I want to sing gospel at an African-American church.

I want to meet my biological father and show him what he has missed out on the last 23 years.

DUNCAN PENN

Right after high school graduation, a bunch of friends and I went camping. It was a classic moving-on trip; we were very happy to be done.

On our last night, my friend Rob accidentally drowned.

I always lived my life expecting to be happy someday, but I had never even really stopped to think what would actually make me happy. I just figured it would happen eventually.

Death has an interesting way of simplifying life. Fears, worries, and pride seem to fall away. You get more courageous and more honest when you're reminded that you're going to die soon. It's that clarity and honesty that help you decide what you want to do with your life.

I hadn't been close to someone who died before Rob, and it really changed me. It pushed me to question what's important to me. Meeting the other guys and forming The Buried Life grew out of that. I'd like to remember Rob and the lesson he taught me.

- -

Duncan Penn is a cofounder of The Buried Life, producer, and publisher.

Before I die, I would like a $\dfrac{\text{SECOND}}{1}$ chance.

I WANT TO CUT DOWN A TREE AND TURN IT INTO A TABLE AND TWO CHAIRS..

"LIFE MOVES PRETTY FAST.
IF YOU DON'T STOP AND LOOK AROUND ONCE
IN A WHILE, YOU COULD MISS IT."
—FERRIS BUELLER

I Want To Write A Book And Catch Someone In A Café or On A Park Bench Reading It !

i just want to have a story worth telling.

I want to sneak into a five-star restaurant dressed as a waiter and serve people.

BEFORE I DIE,
I WANT to
PUT HOGWARTS
ADMISSION
LETTERS
INTO AS
MANY
MAILBOXES
AS POSSIBLE.

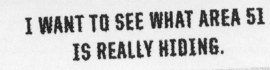

I WANT TO SEE WHAT AREA 51
IS REALLY HIDING.

"MANY OF LIFE'S FAILURES ARE PEOPLE WHO DID NOT REALIZE HOW CLOSE THEY WERE TO SUCCESS WHEN THEY GAVE UP."

—THOMAS EDISON

I WANT TO GO ON AN
ADVENTURE WITH MY
BROTHERS JONNIE AND
DUNCAN AND MY LITTLE
SISTER—TAKE A
ROAD TRIP, OR BACKPACK
THROUGH EUROPE, OR
VISIT A DESERT ISLAND,
OR SEE THE GULF ISLANDS.

I want to build my mom

the most amazing house so
she CAN finally have the home
she deserves.

I WANT TO FOIL A ROBBERY.

BE THE HERO. SHAKE HANDS WITH THE MAYOR. :)

BEFORE I DIE I WANT TO MEET THE NYC POLICE OFFICER WHO DELIVERED ME IN MY PARENTS' BATHROOM BECAUSE THERE WAS NO TIME TO GET TO THE HOSPITAL.

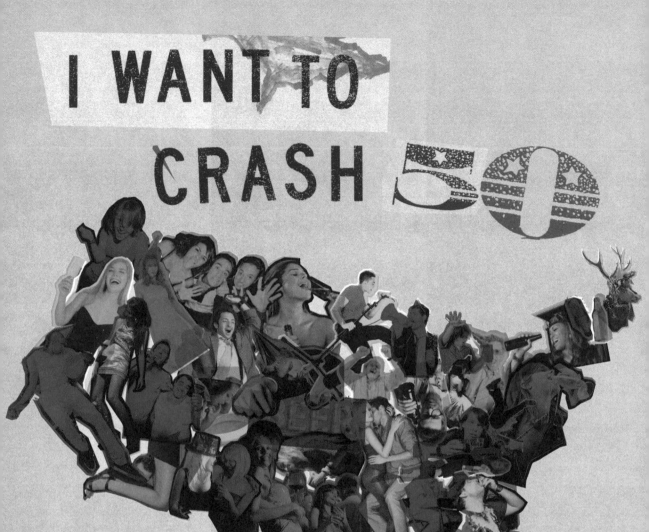

I WANT TO CRASH 50 PARTIES IN 50 STATES.

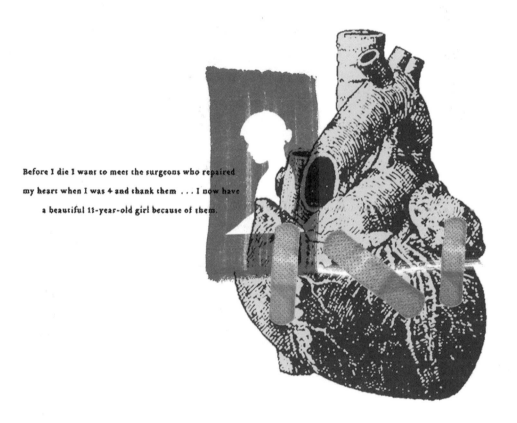

Before I die I want to meet the surgeons who repaired my heart when I was 4 and thank them . . . I now have a beautiful 11-year-old girl because of them.

I WAN
SWIM IN

T TO JELL-O.

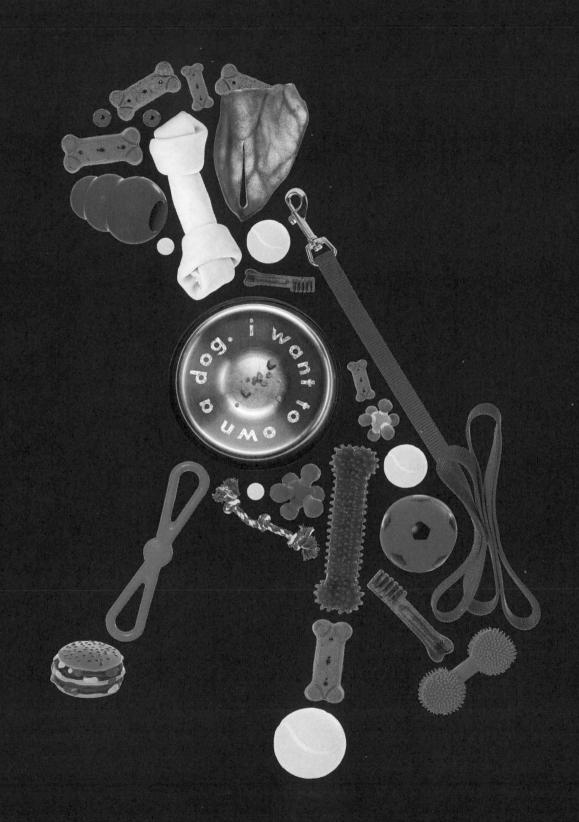

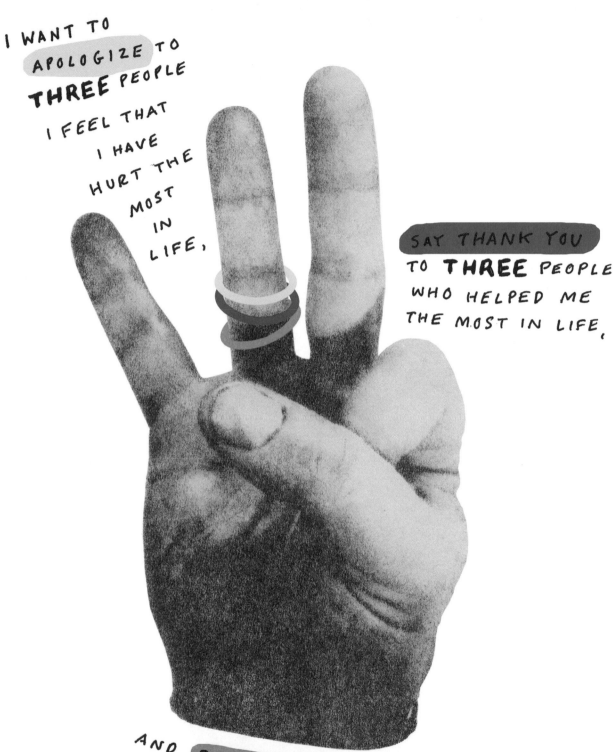

"IT WAS ALL A DREAM."
—THE NOTORIOUS B.I.G.

I WANT TO HAVE MY FIRST KISS

i want to convince the person i love the most— my best friend my boyfriend my everything—that life isn't all about making money. The love we share is worth the sacrifice. That happiness has no dollar $ign.

I want to Model
In New York! :)

I want to find my unrelated twin

I want to take a year and grow everything I eat.

I want to find my birth mom and thank her for giving me the best life I could have and for loving me enough to give me a family that could provide what I needed.

CUSTOM MADE IN THE USA

"I'M LIVIN' LIFE RIGHT NOW, MAN.
AND THIS IS WHAT I'MA DO TILL IT'S OVER."
—DRAKE

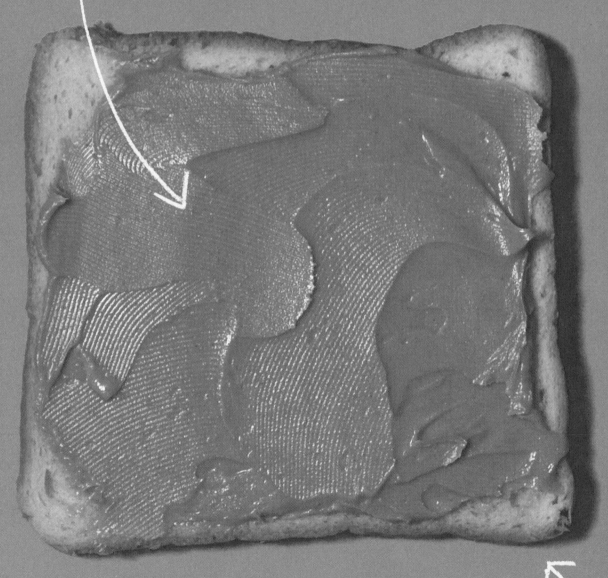

I want to have
a threesome

with John Stamos

and
Sandra
Bullock.

I want to share my artwork with The World.

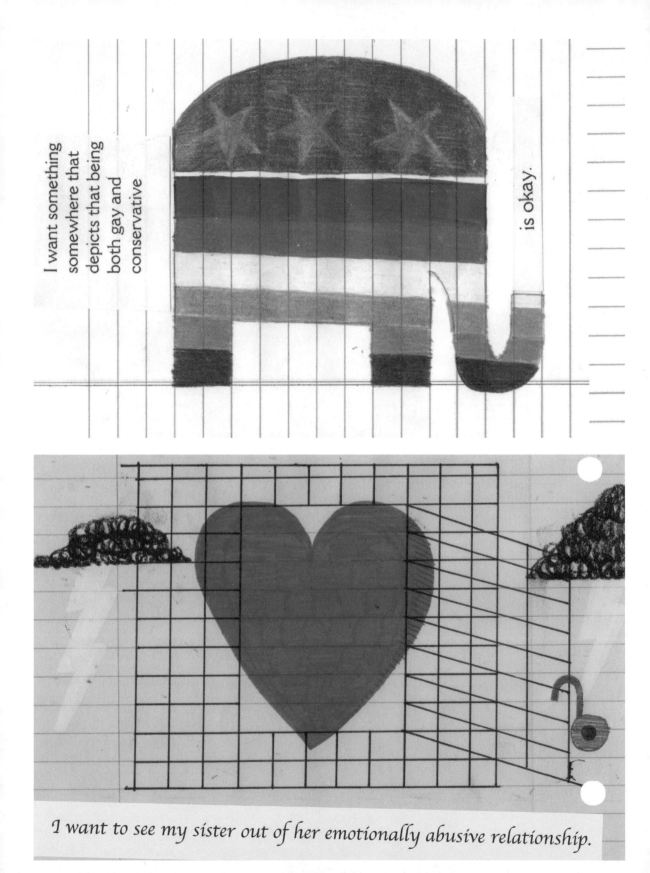

I want something somewhere that depicts that being both gay and conservative is okay.

I want to see my sister out of her emotionally abusive relationship.

"WE ARE ALL IN THE GUTTER, BUT SOME OF US ARE LOOKING AT THE STARS."

—OSCAR WILDE

I WANT TO WALK INTO A BUILDING THAT I HAVE DESIGNED.

I WANT TO FARM MY OWN LAND.

I want to go to a cemetery and put a flower on every grave.

I WANT TO MAKE
FOOTPRINTS ON THE MOON.

DAVE LINGWOOD

The opportunity to work as an assistant guide in Namibia at my uncle's Wild Dog Safari—my dream job—had landed in my lap. Watching people's reactions the first time they spotted lions roaming through the tall grass was awesome, and despite the fact that I had to rise at 5:00 A.M. to make my boss coffee, I loved my job. We should note—a morning person, I am not.

I guess the early-morning coffee fetching got to me eventually. After a three-month stint in Africa, I found myself in Lethbridge, Alberta, enrolled in a university. Not exactly thrilled at the thought of swapping safari tours and elephants for a school in small-town-prairie Canada, I decided to be "That Guy" you see in every college movie. I had a fully stocked bar and the sickest sound system in my dorm.

Hour twenty-two of college life: I woke up to a security guard nudging me in the dorm foyer. I was naked with a small towel wrapped around me and apparently had forgotten the entry code to the building. After kindly thanking the guard, I decided to have a shower and perhaps a quick nap before my first class. When I looked in the mirror, I saw that—to my surprise—a flaming shooter had burned off my left eyebrow.

So it continued. Five to seven nights a week, I was stumbling drunk. After eight months existing on twelve-packs and cafeteria food, my badonkadonk was so large that my nickname, D. Lo, had stuck. I was forty-five pounds heavier than when I arrived. My grades were terrible and continued to get worse. I had to start withdrawing from courses.

"Jenna, I'm so sorry for peeing on your door. I have cleaned everything around it and even shampooed the carpet. I'm so sorry. —Dave." Messages like this became more frequent. When my dry-erase scribble became recognizable to everyone in my dorm, I knew my drinking was out of hand.

The second semester was in full swing. I was depressed and battling severe social anxiety. Talking to others was really uncomfortable—I constantly felt like I was squirming in my own skin. Deep down I began to realize that this behavior was surface noise for what was really going on underneath. I needed to do something about it; I just didn't know what.

When I got home, my friend Olivier greeted me with "Holy shit, you're fat." A dapper East Indian dude, Olivier was the kind of guy who would host a party, break a beer bottle over his head with a smile, and then wake up the next morning at six to give a speech on social change to a board of directors. He usually answers the phone in a rush: "Hey, man. I just got back from a fifteen-mile run and I'm about to sit down and compose the musical score for this new screenplay I'm working on. But what's up?"

His overachieving personality could have been overwhelming if he weren't such a good guy. Olivier became my very own Tony Robbins.

One night we spent eight hours talking. For the first time, I opened up and told him that my life was unraveling. I was depressed and miserable. Olivier shook his head and nailed it with zero pity: "It sounds like you just wasted an entire year of your life." And I had.

He fired questions at me: "Where do you want to be in ten years? What does that look like? Who do you most admire? Who blows your mind?"

For the first time in years, dreams, passion, inspiration, and a faint surge of hope came over me. It was a dull sensation, but I liked it. There was something to look forward to in my future. We sat in an '81 Volvo all night. I can still hear the song by Broken Social Scene playing on repeat. By 3:00 A.M., I had a page of notes and Olivier was assigning homework. I was going to get my grades up, I would go after what made me happy, and of course I had to go for a run—stat.

Olivier kept me in check and made sure that everything I committed to or said I wanted to do, I did—small steps in the right direction. The first year of my college journey was selfish. I was slacking, lazy, and running away. Olivier's "You have no one to blame but yourself" model slapped me in the face, and it finally hit me that I could choose the life I wished to lead. If I wanted to change, it would need to come from within. By the end of the first semester of my second year, I was earning A's and B's—the highest grades I'd ever gotten. I taught break dancing three days a week, and I lost all but my freshman fifteen. Most important, I was happy, passionate, and excited about my future rather than worried. It was a Tuesday in February when I got a phone call about a new opportunity. It was my friend Jonnie, arranging a meeting with some guys from back home about a film project.

- -

Dave Lingwood is a cofounder of The Buried Life, producer, and comedian.

I want to tell my parents that I love them.

"BE KIND, FOR EVERYONE YOU MEET
IS FIGHTING A BATTLE YOU KNOW
NOTHING ABOUT."

—WENDY MASS

I want to finally say good-bye to my four friends who were killed in a car accident.

I want to Witness A Miracle

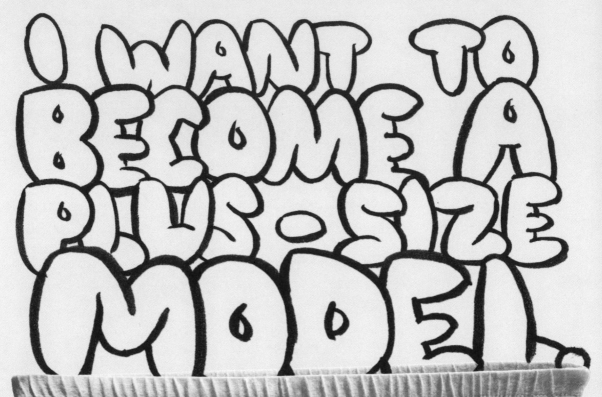

The POWER of
Your Subconscious Mind

Joseph Murphy

D.R.S., D.D., Ph.D., LL.D.
Fellow of the Andhra Research
University of India

I WANT TO
READ SOMEONE'S
MIND.

BANTAM BOOKS
NEW YORK · TORONTO · LONDON · SYDNEY · AUCKLAND

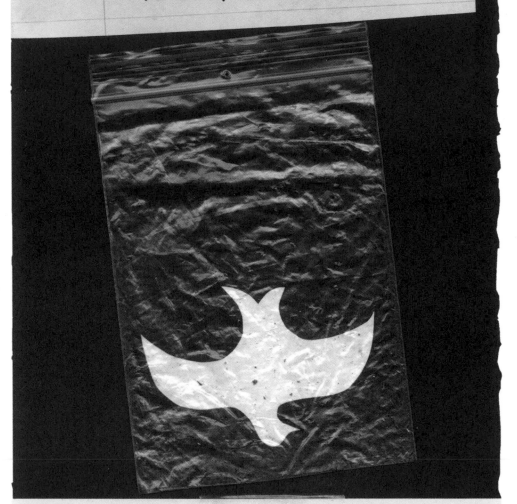

I WANT TO FIGURE OUT WHO SOLD MY BROTHER THE DRUGS.

R.I.P. SAM HUSTON

I want to rappel off Mount Rushmore.

I WANT TO
BE A MAN.

I WANT

NOT TO
BE SCARED

TO LET MYSELF

FALL
HEAD OVER
HEELS
IN LOVE
AGAIN.

I WANT TO WALK AWAY FROM AN EXPLOSION

IN SLOW MOTION.

I want to have a boat named after me.

I want me and my family

to become

American citizens.

**"NEVER TELL ME THE SKY
IS THE LIMIT WHEN THERE ARE
FOOTPRINTS ARE ON THE MOON."**
—ANONYMOUS

I want to take

a cute girl

to the

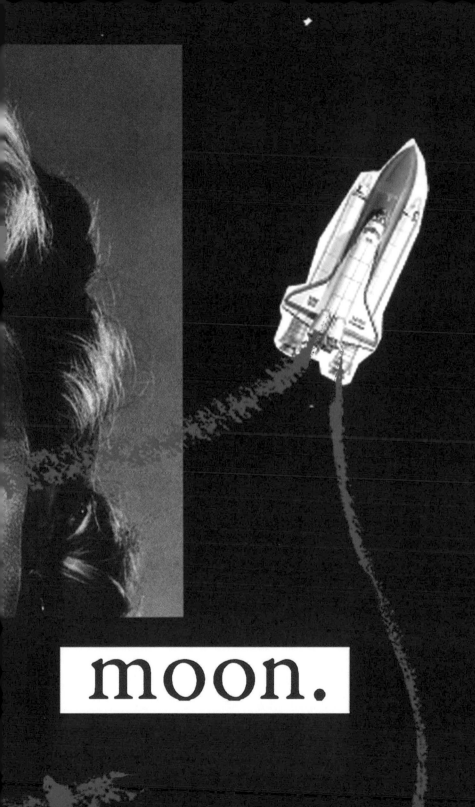

moon.

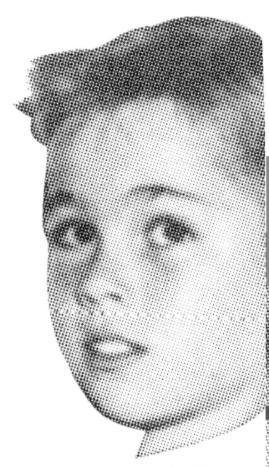

I <u>WAN</u>T to go to a city where NOBODY knows me...

...AND ACT like a COMPLETELY DIFFERENT PERSON.

I want to get my parents

out of debt.

I WANT TO FEEL WHAT IT'S LIKE TO USE MY LEGS.

JONNIE PENN

When I first stepped into our musky 1977 Dodge Coachman RV, ready to hit the road on that initial Buried Life adventure, I wondered about a few things.

I wondered about the night that our friend Rob died, and about the gap it must have left for his family. I wondered about my brother, Duncan, who was with him. I wondered if other cultures prepared each other for the pain of losing someone. I wondered if we cherished life without understanding it. I wondered if college felt like a factory to anybody else. I wondered why our generation didn't protest more. I wondered why George W. Bush was the American president. I wondered if my parents would stay divorced. I wondered why people worry so much about what others think. I wondered if I was in love with a girl named Lorena. I wondered how I'd pay for college the next year. I wondered if I'd make it onto the debate team. I wondered about having fun in Victoria. I wondered if I would do well on my exams that year. I wondered if that guy Aaron was serious about starting a band. I wondered about breaking loose. I wondered about that one party, when the deck collapsed. I wondered if my big sis was having fun. I wondered about Adbusters. I wondered about activism. I wondered why we worry so much if we know life is temporary. I wondered if my friends in Montreal would like my new friend Dave. I wondered how much money I had left for groceries. I wondered why my neighbor Ben kept calling me even though we didn't know each other that well. I wondered if I should have more courage. I wondered how all this would go, being out on the road together in an RV we'd been told was going to go up in flames. I wondered if I was going to feel better by the time we were we done with our summer road trip. I wondered how many times I'd had strep throat that year. I wondered why more people didn't rebel. I wondered if my other sister was ever going to have a wild streak. I wondered if her boyfriend liked the shoes I gave him. I wondered if this project was going to change my life. I wondered if we'd make a documentary one day. I wondered about how Matthew Arnold felt when he wrote "The Buried Life." I wondered if he knew he'd be dead soon. I wondered why some guys bought *GQ* magazine. I wondered if I'd be rich one day. I wondered if I'd be able to help someone. I wondered if I'd be happier. I wondered if life was as sad as it seemed for so many. I wondered if the ones who used hollow words knew it. I wondered if they felt sad about that too. I wondered if they'd join the fight when it needed them. I wondered about you. I wondered if it's better to be honest even when it hurts. I wondered whether if it all ends well, it was worth it. I wondered about details. I wondered about pain. I wondered why we hide from each other. I wondered if death was the only thing that made it okay to be honest. I wondered about antidotes. I wondered about that burn, burn, burn; that fabulous yellow roman candle exploding like a spider across the stars. I wondered if it was time to get up and go now.

Hmm. I expect it was.

Jonnie Penn is a cofounder of The Buried Life, youth rights advocate, artificial intelligence expert, and speaker.

"SOONER OR LATER THE MAN WHO WINS IS THE MAN WHO THINKS HE CAN."

—NAPOLEON HILL

I WANT TO CREW WITH THE
SEA SHEPHERDS AND HELP
SAVE THE WORLD'S OCEANS.

I WANT TO FIND MY MOM A BOYFRIEND.*

* AND I WANT HIM TO TREAT HER RIGHT, TOO!

Bella Brunell-Cochran ▶
Stephen Childs

I want to be sure that my husband knows just how much I love him...that there is nothing else in the entire world that has or ever could make me even the slightest bit as happy as he makes me every single second.

28 days ago · Comment · Like · Dislike · Reconsider · Fast Forward · Contemplate in Silence

 You and 814 other people like this.

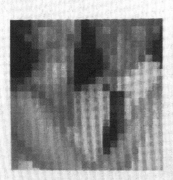

Bella Brunell-Cochran ▶
Stephen Childs

I want to be sure that my husband knows just how much I love him...that there is nothing else in the entire world that has or ever could make me even the slightest

I WANT TO SEE MY SISTER OVERCOME HER ANXIETY. SHE'S ONLY 18 AND HAS BARELY LEFT THE HOUSE IN 4 YEARS.

I

want

to

believe

in

God.

"WHEN I DO GOOD, I FEEL GOOD.
WHEN I DO BAD, I FEEL BAD.
THAT'S MY RELIGION."
—ABRAHAM LINCOLN

I want to fall in love one more time. Even though I am married to the last person I fell in love with. Even though I am committed to the marriage.

BEFORE I DIE

I WANT TO FIND

THE GIRL I FELL

IN LOVE WITH ON

A SHORT FLIGHT.

I want to save someone who is trapped in a burning building.

1. B. Murray

2. D. Aykroyd

I want to meet
the Ghostbusters.

3. H. Ramis

4. E. Hudson

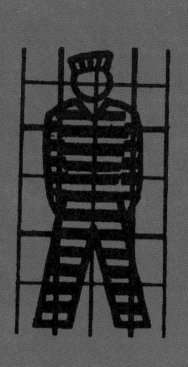

I want my dad to be on the other side of the bars without the orange jumpsuit.

I WANT MY PARENTS TO SAY,

"THAT'S MY DAUGHTER."

"IT'S NEVER TOO LATE TO BE WHAT YOU MIGHT HAVE BEEN."

—GEORGE ELIOT

I want to
toboggan
down

a double
black
diamond.

I

no longer

want to

be afraid

of the dark.

I WANT TO COVER THE ENTIRE
FLOOR OF MY GIRLFRIEND'S HOUSE
IN CHOCOLATE KISSES SO I CAN SAY,
"I KISS THE GROUND YOU WALK ON."

I WANT TO RAISE HELL

"STAY HUNGRY. STAY FOOLISH."
—STEWART BRAND

I want to go around the world in 80 days in a hot-air balloon!

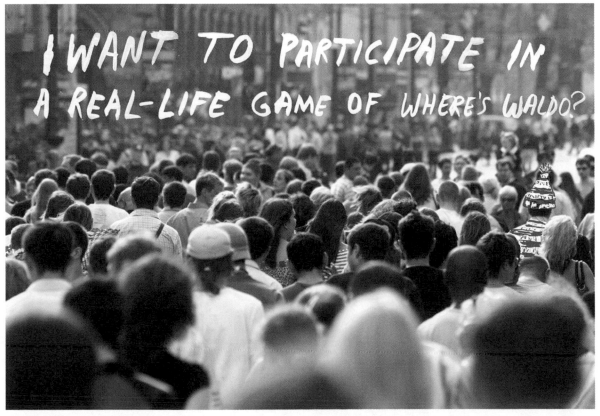

I WANT TO PARTICIPATE IN A REAL-LIFE GAME OF WHERE'S WALDO?

i want to be

COMPLETELY

and...

BLISSFULLY

:) HAPPY :)

I WANT TO CREATE AND NAME A NEW COLOR CRAYON.

I want to make a mark.

THANK YOU

Our most sincere thanks to all of our friends and family; to our hometown of Victoria, British Columbia; to the few special individuals who taught us that dreams can become a reality; to the hardworking artists who gave the project form and a structure; to the young people around the world who fuel The Buried Life. We're honored to have been able to make this journey with you.

BEN, DAVE, DUNCAN, JONNIE

Hope you enjoyed our book. Mischief managed.